ONE CRAZY DAY

The Story from Mozart's Marriage of Figaro

Told by
Richard Morris

Illustrated by
Hatty Morris and Sayaka Takeuchi

Copyright © 2013 Richard Morris
All rights reserved.

ISBN: 1490389210
ISBN-13: 9781490389219

Also by Richard Morris and Hatty Morris

The Nibelung Ballad: the story from Wagner's Ring

CONTENTS

Introduction vii

Act 1 1

Act 2 13

Act 3 33

Act 4 45

INTRODUCTION

For many people, Mozart's *The Marriage of Figaro* is the perfect opera. It was composed by Mozart at the very summit of his extraordinary powers in the space of a month or two in 1785 and had its first performance in Vienna the following year.

The story of the opera derives from the play *La Folle Journée ou Le Mariage de Figaro*, written by Mozart's contemporary, Beaumarchais, in 1781 and first performed by the Comedie Francaise in Paris in 1784. Beaumarchais was an adventurer, a writer and above all a libertarian, and his play is imbued with the spirit of freedom and equality that led to the French Revolution a few years later. It is a real-life story depicting a great range of emotional connections between the characters and, in this sense, strongly at odds with the then dominant Enlightenment philosophy of the supremacy of reason.

The play was also radical in asserting the equal rights of master and servant; the rights of women and the capacity of women to act in alliance. It is deeply critical of dissolute aristocracy. As a result, the play underwent no less that six censorships, before being finally approved for performance by King Louis XVI. Similarly, the opera was initially banned, before being finally approved for performance by Emperor Joseph II.

The opera is the first of the three great collaborations between Mozart and his librettist, Lorenzo da Ponte, their subsequent operas being *Don Giovanni* and *Cosi fan Tutte*. The two men shared both the radicalism and the story-telling power of Beaumarchais. *The Marriage of Figaro* is a brilliant play, brilliantly adapted as a libretto and miraculously set to music.

INTRODUCTION

The plot is extremely complex and the purpose of this slim volume is to tell the story as clearly and concisely as is consistent with the inclusion of all relevant details. Many people who have heard and seen the opera many times are still unsure of all the twists and turns. This book is for them as much as for those approaching this masterpiece for the first time.

Musically, the opera is bursting with ensembles, all of which move the action forward with relentless pace and great intensity. The characters and their individual stories are expressed musically in the most innovatory way, demonstrating profound psychological insights. The music heightens not just the drama, but also the sense that good will ultimately prevail; thus, the surprise appearance of Susanna and the Countess at critical moments gives a feeling of something close to salvation.

So, telling the story from the opera has very special challenges. I have chosen the *terza rima* form, with its interwoven rhyming scheme, to reflect best the interwoven strands of the plot; and have introduced sprung rhythms to accelerate the pace at moments of special intensity, particularly those involving the agitated page boy, Cherubino. In both the poetry and the illustrations we have sought to convey something of the energy, pace, wit and *joie de vivre* of this magnificent opera; and, in lines 124 and 274, that sense of divine intervention.

The action of the opera is set in the country house of Count and Countess Almaviva at Aguasfrescas, near Seville. The action is contemporaneous with the first performances of the play and the opera themselves. For the original audiences, therefore, the opera was a mirror of their own lives. The entire action, over four Acts, takes place within one crazy day.

INTRODUCTION

It is important, before the curtain goes up, to know two outcomes from Beaumarchais' prequel, *The Barber of Seville*. First, Count Almaviva has won Rosina from the clutches of Doctor Bartolo (whose ward she was), with the assistance of the barber, Figaro. The Count has subsequently married Rosina, so she is his Countess, and has engaged Figaro as his valet. Secondly, the Count has recently abolished the *Droit de Seigneur*, which had entitled him to sleep with any of his female servants immediately before their marriage. No doubt his repeal of this right was enacted in the spirit of love for his new wife and of emerging liberalism. His marriage, however, has run into difficulty and he bitterly regrets his decision.

Now please study the list of Characters and read on.

Richard Morris

July 2013

CHARACTERS

Count Almaviva, *a Spanish nobleman*

Countess Almaviva, *his wife*

Susanna, *the Countess's maid, engaged to Figaro*

Figaro, *the Count's valet*

Cherubino, *the Count's page*

Marcellina, *housekeeper to Doctor Bartolo*

Doctor Bartolo, *a doctor from Seville*

Don Basilio, *a music teacher*

Don Curzio, *a lawyer*

Barberina, *daughter of Antonio*

Antonio, *a gardener, uncle of Susanna*

ACT I

ACT I

Scenes 1 - 4

While Figaro is measuring the room,

Susanna's trying on her wedding hat

and needs the full attention of her groom.

But when he tells her, at her bidding, that

the room's for them, she reads beneath the text   5

and knows at once their ship is heading at

the rocks, for their married quarters will be next

to the bedroom of their lord, Count Almaviva;

they've known for long the Count is over-sexed,

now her man must wake up and believe her: 10

she his future wife's become the target

for seduction by this carnal high achiever.

ACT I

The valet Figaro resolves to get

the better of the womanising Count.

The battle-lines between the two are set.   15

Figaro must furthermore account

to Marcellina, by paying back a loan

or, if he cannot pay *the said amount*,

by marrying her. Bartolo is shown

the contract and revels in the chance to gain   20

revenge on him and riddance of the crone.

Marcellina rudely tries to feign

subservience to Susanna, who repays

her spite and triumphs in the hate campaign.

Marcellina exits, eyes ablaze.   25

ACT I

Scenes 5 - 7

The page Cherubino, confused adolescent, appears

in a hurry to confide in Susanna he's been caught

by the Count with her cousin, Barberina. Now he fears

he may be dismissed from the house and is utterly distraught

as he loves every woman there, most of all the Countess;   30

endlessly speaking of love, his mind's overwrought.

They are caught unawares as their lecherous master pounces.

The pageboy hides behind a chair, as the Count sets out

to seduce Susanna, who staunchly won't pronounce *Yes*.

Basilio, who fawns on the Count, is heard without.   35

The Count makes a move to hide behind the chair, so the page

creeps round to the front and onto the seat, just about

ACT I

in time for Susanna to cover the hapless, teenage

lover with a dress, before Basilio enters.

He tries to pimp for the Count, ignoring her rage, 40

and insinuates the page is not only her lover but hankers

for the Countess. The Count's so angry at such an improper

idea he emerges. Susanna's overcome by her tormentors,

who, as they help her to a chair, try to grope her.

She repulses them both and refutes the charges. "Be in no 45

doubt", says the Count, "the page is a known interloper.

Yesterday someone was with Barberina. Being so

sure, I lifted a cloth" – he illustrates this

by lifting the dress from the chair – [he gasps] – "Cherubino!"

The Count implies there's a guilty liaison, baseless 50

though this is; he threatens to expose Susanna

to Figaro, but stops when he sees how weak his case is,

the page having heard his own brazen attempt to suborn her.

ACT I

Scene 8

Figaro brings a chorus of peasants he's bribed
to praise the Count for ending the *Droit de Seigneur*,   55
he humbly invites the Count to crown his bride

with a pure white veil to show that she's retained her
virtue. He, however, sensing the ploy,
plays for time and announces he'll arrange a

far finer ceremony, which they'll all enjoy.   60
The peasants depart. The Count decides the page
must go to join his army corps. The boy
is mocked by Figaro, as they leave the stage.

ACT 2

ACT 2

Scenes 1 - 2

The Countess, in her bedroom, feels despair

at her husband's constant promiscuity. 65

Susanna speaks of what they're both aware:

his lust for her and the incongruity

of his jealous vanity about his wife;

but, if Figaro's resolved to do it, he

will find a way to overcome this strife. 70

He enters and ebulliently presents

his plans: he's sent the Count an unsigned brief,

ACT 2

via Basilio, with bogus evidence
his wife will meet a lover later; the ruse
will occupy his thoughts from this time hence   75

until the Count no longer can refuse
to seal the match of Figaro and Susanna;
to cap it all, Susanna should confuse

the Count still more by showing, through her manner,
a willingness to meet him in the garden;   80
they'll dress up Cherubino as a woman – her

replacement – so he'll have to ask for pardon
from the Countess, when she finds them *in flagrante*.
Figaro departs. He's soon far gone,
still certain he'll emerge triumphantly.   85

ACT 2

Scenes 3 – 4

A forlorn Cherubino enters the room soon after.
He sings to the women about his tormented heart –
is it love that I feel? he enquires. Restraining their laughter,

they check that he knows of Figaro's plans, then start
on a dress rehearsal, first locking the door. He shows 90
the Countess his army commission and, being alert,

she observes the seal is missing. Susanna then goes
through the door at the back in search of a suitable dress,
leaving her mistress alone with the page, in the throes

of his grief at having to part. In a state of undress 95
he asks for a kiss... a knock at the door... it's her husband!
Cherubino, aghast, at a loss, and under duress,
locks himself into the Countess's dressing-room and...

ACT 2

Scenes 5 – 8

in fear, the Countess opens the door to her room.
The Count asks why the door was locked, then makes   100
her read the unsigned letter. He's bound to assume

she's with a lover; noise from the dressing-room wakes
his suspicion. The Countess says Susanna's inside
and tells her not to come out, thus raising the stakes.

Just then Susanna returns; she's able to hide   105
and sees the Count about to summon his men
to force the door, intent on homicide.

Instead, he locks all other doors, and then
compels his wife to go with him to fetch
some tools, so he can force the dressing-room open   110

ACT 2

himself. At once, Susanna calls to the wretch-
ed page to escape. He emerges, out of his wits,
and leaps from the window into the vegetable patch.

Susanna laughs, resolving she'll be quits
with the Count, as she takes the place of the escapee   115
and her Lord and Lady return with drill and bits.

The Countess thinks the game is up, so she
admits the detainee is not her maid
but Cherubino, half-undressed... the three
of them had planned a harmless masquerade...   120

Scene 9

The furious Count declares that she is faithless
and he will kill the page. Seizing the key,
he barges open the dressing-room door and faces

ACT 2

Susanna.

The Count and Countess are equally baffled; he   125
takes time to search the room and, in that frame,
the maid shows her the route of the escapee.

The Count returns and asks for pardon; their game,
he says, was cruel; but his wife and Susanna refuse
to grant it; the crime was his, he's wholly to blame.   130

He asks them about the unsigned letter: who's
the author? They admit, as part of the joke,
Figaro wrote it. The Count repents, his abuse
is forgiven and peace returns to the gentlefolk.

ACT 2

Scenes 10 -12

Figaro enters in buoyant spirits to gather   135
them all for the wedding. The Count demurs to enquire
if Figaro knows who wrote the unsigned letter.

Ignoring prompts and brazenly acting the liar,
the valet denies all knowledge. They plead with their Lord
to approve the marriage and grant their deepest desire.   140

ACT 2

Just then Antonio enters and staggers toward
the Count, complaining his plants have been destroyed
by a man who fell, or was thrown, from the balcony overboard

into the garden. Figaro, knowing the boy had
jumped, tells the Count to pay no attention, 145
the gardener's drunk, his claims are totally void.

But when Antonio sticks to his story, tension
mounts and Figaro says it was he who jumped,
in panic on hearing the shouts and angry dissension.

Antonio proffers the papers the jumper had dumped, 150
but these are seized by the Count, who asks his valet
what they are, and promptly dismisses the unkempt

gardener. Figaro waits and is able to calculate,
helped by the women, it must be the page's commission.
The Count asks why the boy had passed him this billet. 155

ACT 2

Figaro's dumb, but the women are in a position
to whisper the answer. The Count's confounded when told
by his man of the need for a seal, and its omission.

At this moment, to the Count's delight, old
Marcellina, her counsel Bartolo and witness Basilio   160
enter the room to petition their Lord to uphold

her contract of marriage to Figaro, as judge ex-officio
in this case. Figaro, Susanna and the Countess
are stunned by this turn of events, which cause an imbroglio
whose outcome none can foresee or, even less, guess.   165

ACT 3

ACT 3

Scenes 1 - 4

The Count is puzzled as he ponders the events of the day.
Susanna comes in, on the pretext of running an errand
for her Lady; demurely she signals she's up for a rendez-

vous later that day in the garden. The Count, impassioned
at first, becomes suspicious, when he hears her confide   170
in Figaro soon after. He vows he will never play second
fiddle to his servant and their knot will never be tied.

Scenes 5 - 6

The lawyer, Don Curzio, decides the case. His verdict
is: *pay up or marry her.* Figaro claims he cannot
be married without the consent of his parents – a perfect   175

defence, because he was stolen at birth and has got
no idea who they are; the only clue is a spatula
mark on his arm. Marcellina exclaims: *a what?!*

ACT 3

She discloses to Figaro news that is truly spectacular:

he is her long-lost son and his father is Bartolo.   180

The Count is stunned, for him it's a blow to the jugular;

for them, a time to embrace and happily wallow

in newly-found love. Just then Susanna appears

with money she's raised for her fellow, but simply can't swallow

ACT 3

the sight of him kissing her rival. She boxes his ears. 185
But, on learning the truth, her anger's converted to bliss:
two couples will marry, the young ones and the old dears,
and none of them cares the Count may take things amiss.

Scenes 7 - 14

The Countess is anxious to hear how her husband replied
to Susanna's advances. She feels disgraced, but knows 190
she loves him still and wants him back by her side.

Susanna reports on all there is to disclose.
The Countess dictates an amorous letter for her
to give to the Count to confirm their date and propose

ACT 3

the meeting be under the pine trees. To add an aura   195
of mystery, they seal the note with a pin and write
on the back to request its return by the one who adores her.

Barberina arrives with girls from the town, who delight
in presenting bouquets to the Countess. Cherubino, dressed
as a girl, is hidden amongst them. From out of sight   200

Antonio appears with the Count and unmasks the transvestite page, whom the Count then threatens to punish for not having left for the army. Barberina's far from impressed;

expressing the hope the Count could not have forgot
his ardent promise, she begs him to give her the page   205
as husband. Figaro comes to ask everyone what

is keeping them from the party. The Count, in a rage,
suggests he's a liar, saying the page has admitted
it's he who jumped from the window into the cabbage.

ACT 3

The valet retorts, as he jumped down, the quick-witted   210
page could have done the same. When everyone leaves,
the Countess insists her furious husband be seated

to welcome the wedding couples. As he receives
both them and the guests, they praise in song his repeal
of the *Droit de Seigneur*, and Susanna secretly gives   215

him her letter. He pricks his finger on breaking its seal,
proceeds to read it, give it a kiss and conceal
the pin in his sleeve. The Count then invites them all
to come that night to a fabulous meal and ball.

ACT 4

ACT 4

In the garden at night, Barberina stoops to look 220
for something she's dropped. When Figaro comes to her aid,
she divulges she's lost the pin, which she undertook,

on behalf of the Count, to return to the Countess's maid
as *the seal of the pine grove*. Figaro's quite distraught.
He resolves to spy on the couple and in a tirade 225

says he'll avenge all husbands. He gives a report
of all he's learnt to Basilio and to his parents,
but no one is able to give him effective support.

Figaro broods on the wiles of women, the torments
Susanna has caused him. Wearing each other's dresses, 230
she and the Countess arrive. Aware of his presence,

ACT 4

knowing he'll hear her words in the dark, she expresses

desire in rapturous tones to punish her man

for doubting her. Now Cherubino, who's out to possess his

Barberina, appears; he sees a person he's certain's   235

Susanna, starts to flirt and takes her hand.

The Countess, its owner, tries to resist his coercion,

scared the Count will see them and misunderstand.

He arrives precisely as she breaks free, and receives

the page's kiss. He responds with a slap meant to land   240

on the page, but catches his valet instead as he leaves

his lair to see what is up. The page and Figaro

go. The Count, now alone with the one he believes

ACT 4

is Susanna, begins to make love to the wife he'd forgo.

As they retire to hide in the trees, the furious 245

valet, who's also deceived, as a *quid pro quo*

steps into their path, causing the hotly promiscuous

Count to withdraw and his wife to run to a bower

nearby. On seeing Susanna, who he thinks is the virtuous

Countess, Figaro offers the chance to allow her 250

to spy on the Count with his bride. But when she replies,

he instantly knows it is she. Restored to power,

ACT 4

he declares to her his undying love, in her guise

as the Countess. To his delight, she slaps his face

and goes on slapping, until at last he mollifies 255

her by letting her know she couldn't efface

the voice he adores. They embrace and make their peace,

just as the Count returns to resume the chase.

To bring to an end this comical master-piece,

they re-enact the scene, so their jealous Lord 260

believes he sees his wife in a state of bliss

with Figaro. Finding himself without a sword,

he summons his men, as Susanna beats a retreat

to a garden arcade at hand. With one accord

Antonio, Bartolo, Basilio and Curzio entreat 265

the Count to say what's wrong. He's been betrayed,

he says, by Figaro and the Countess's deceit.

ACT 4

He calls for his wife to come out from her arcade,

but first the page, then Barberina, then

old Marcellina come, before the maid, 270

dressed as the Countess, does as she is bidden.

Everyone kneels to ask for her pardon, but he

replies fiercely: *no, no no, and no again!*

ACT 4

The Countess

emerges, reveals herself and joins their plea.　　　　275

The astounded Count, overcome with remorse, kneels

and begs her forgiveness. *Yes* is the answer she

gives him. They all set off to the revelries.

Richard Morris, a former chief executive of ABRSM (Associated Board of the Royal Schools of Music), lawyer, investment banker and publisher, is chairman of the Yehudi Menuhin School and deputy chairman of the Mayor of London's Fund for Young Musicians. He has been a regular opera-goer for a great number of years and an occasional opera-singer for a few of them. He has served as a trustee of Kent Opera and was co-founder of Almaviva Opera. He studies and writes poetry and is an associate director of Magma Poetry.

Hatty Morris is a freelance artist and designer, having graduated from Cambridge University and from the City and Guilds of London Art School. During 2011/12 she was a member of the design team for the Opening and Closing Ceremonies of the London Olympic and Paralympic Games.

Sayaka Takeuchi studied Landscape Architecture and Interior Design and trained at various design companies. She produces spatial design, including interior and set, and provides art direction and prop making for a variety of media.